BECOMING THE

CONFIDENT

PRESENTER

A COMPLETE GUIDE ON HOW TO
DITCH YOUR SPEECH ANXIETY AND
UNLOCK THE SECRETS TO HIGHLY
EFFECTIVE SPEAKING AND
PRESENTATION SKILLS

Hudson Jose

TABLE OF CONTENT

There are three things to aim at in public speaking: first, to get into your subject, then to get your subject into yourself, and lastly, to get your subject into the heart of your audience." Alexander Gregg.

THE POWER OF CONFIDENT COMMUNICATION

"The success of your presentation will be judged not by the knowledge you send but by what the listener receives. " Lilly Walters

In a world driven by connectivity and ideas, the ability to articulate thoughts, inspire minds, and move hearts is an invaluable skill. It's a skill that cut across professions, industries, and cultures, a skill that can propel careers, ignite movements, and leave an everlasting impression on the fabric of society.

Welcome to the world of confident speaking, where words have the power to inspire revolutions, form friendships, and bring dreams to life. Picture this: an audience on the edge of their seats, their eyes wide with interest, their minds wide open to new possibilities. This is the power of successful communication, the power contained inside every word uttered with conviction, clarity, and purpose.

But let's take a step back.

Close your eyes and recall a time when you felt a surge of adrenaline as you stood in front of an audience. Perhaps it was in a meeting room full of eager faces, or on a stage drenched in spotlights, with every pair of eyes fixed on you. Do you remember the knot in your gut, your beating heart, and your clammy hands? The universal reality is that fear of public speaking is pervasive, casting a great shadow over countless people regardless of experience or competence.

Why, you may question, does this dread have such a strong hold on us?

The solution is hidden deep inside our human mind. Our forefathers huddled around fireplaces millennia ago, telling stories of survival and wisdom. The speaker possessed not simply words in those times, but the whole essence of knowledge and leadership. Fast forward to now, and while the setting has changed, but the essence remains unchanged. The urge to express ideas, shape attitudes, and make an impression endures. We begin on this trip along with this desire and the obstacles that stand in its way.

Hudson Jose is my name, and I've been where you are. I've felt the flutter of nervousness before stepping onto the stage, and I've dealt the maze of uncertainties that every speaker faces. Over the last 25 years, I've dedicated myself to the art and science of public speaking, not only as a business tycoon, but as a devoted student of the craft.

This book is the result of my experiences, achievements, and hard-earned lessons garnered from innumerable presentations, stages conquered, and audiences moved. But it's also a guide, a guiding light for you, the aspiring speaker, the seasoned presenter looking for improvement, or the corporate executive seeking that compelling presence during high-stakes meetings.

Within these pages, we'll unravel the mysteries of captivating content creation, delve into the complexities of delivery techniques, and decode the secrets of engaging an audience. Together, we'll confront the anxieties that have held many people back and unlock the gates to unwavering confidence in your voice.

But keep in mind that, this journey is not just about acquiring skills; it's about embracing a mindset that views each speaking opportunity as a chance to inspire, to influence, and to leave a lasting impression.

So, are you ready to embark on this life-changing journey? Are you prepared to shed the shackles of speech anxiety and unveil the confident speaker within you?

Turn the page, take a deep breath, and let's begin.

My words have power, and I speak with clarity and confidence

CHAPTER 1: LAYING THE FOUNDATION

"Great speakers are not born, they're trained." Dale Carnegie

Laying a firm foundation is critical in the journey to become a confident speaker. Mastering the principles of public speaking, like the robust base of a building that supports its soaring height, is the cornerstone of your path towards eloquence, influence, and impact.

Understanding and overcoming speech anxiety

The trembling hands, the racing heartbeat, the knots in the stomach, these are the telltale signs of a universal human experience: the fear of public speaking. But fear, my fellow orator, is not an insurmountable mountain; it's a hurdle waiting to be conquered, an obstacle that, once understood, can be harnessed to fuel your journey toward confident speaking.

Speech anxiety, also known as glossophobia, is the fear or nervousness associated with speaking in front of an audience. It's one of the most common fears globally, affecting a sizeable proportion of the population to varied degrees.

Unveiling the Roots of Speech Anxiety

At its core, speech anxiety often stems from a primal fear which is the fear of judgment, rejection, or failure. It's the fear of being seen, heard, and evaluated, it transcends logic and reason, often gripping even the most seasoned speakers.

Fear of Judgment and Rejection: The fear of being judged or rejected by the audience is a significant factor. People worry about making mistakes, being perceived negatively, or facing criticism, leading to anxiety.

Lack of Confidence or Self-Esteem: Individuals with low self-confidence or self-esteem might doubt their abilities to deliver a speech effectively. This lack of belief in oneself contributes to anxiety about public speaking.

Past Negative Experiences: Previous traumatic or embarrassing experiences while speaking in public can linger in the subconscious, creating a fear of repeating those experiences, intensifying anxiety.

Perfectionism: The desire for flawless performance can amplify anxiety. The pressure to meet impossibly high standards leads to fear of failure or making errors during the speech.

Concerns About Being Unprepared: Feeling unprepared or under-rehearsed can trigger anxiety. Individuals worry about forgetting important points or losing track of their speech, leading to anxiety about being exposed.

Physical Symptoms and Performance Anxiety: Fear of visible physical symptoms like sweating, trembling, or stumbling over words can create a cycle of anxiety. The fear of the audience noticing these symptoms intensifies nervousness.

Lack of Control: Feeling like the situation is beyond one's control contributes to anxiety. The fear of unexpected circumstances or an unresponsive audience adds to the stress of public speaking.

Public Speaking as an Unfamiliar Situation: For many, public speaking is a relatively unfamiliar or infrequent activity. Lack of practice or exposure to such situations can exacerbate anxiety.

Understanding the root causes helps individuals tackle their specific fears and develop coping mechanisms to manage and reduce speech anxiety over time.

Strategies to Dismantle Speech Anxiety

Systematic Preparation: Preparation is the cornerstone of confidence. Break down your speech into manageable sections and rehearse them individually. Familiarize yourself with the material until it becomes second nature. Visualize the scenario, envisioning success with each practice session.

Mindfulness and Breathing Techniques: Harness the power of mindfulness. Prior to speaking engagements, practice deep breathing exercises to calm the nerves. Focus on the present moment, acknowledging nervous sensations without judgment. Redirect your thoughts towards positivity and empowerment.

Cognitive Reframing: Challenge negative thoughts and perceptions about speaking. Instead of viewing it as a daunting task, reframe it as an opportunity to share knowledge, inspire, or connect with your audience. Visualize success and positive outcomes.

Exposure and Gradual Desensitization: Start small and build your way up. Begin with low-pressure speaking situations, such as speaking to friends or in smaller group settings. Gradually expose yourself to larger audiences or more challenging scenarios. Each successful experience will bolster your confidence.

Embrace Imperfection: Understand that perfection is an unattainable standard. Embrace the authenticity of imperfection. Instead of fearing mistakes, view them as stepping stones toward improvement. Allow yourself the freedom to learn and grow from every speaking opportunity.

Visualization and Positive Affirmations: Envision success. Picture yourself delivering your speech confidently and captivating your audience. Use positive affirmations, repeat phrases that reinforce your confidence and capability. Affirm your worthiness to speak and influence others positively.

Seek Support and Feedback: Share your speeches or practice sessions with trusted friends, mentors, or speaking groups. Constructive feedback can provide valuable insights and help identify areas for improvement. Accept feedback as a means to refine your skills, not as criticism.

Celebrate Small Wins: Acknowledge and celebrate your victories, no matter how small they may seem. Every successful speech, every moment of overcoming anxiety, is a step forward in your journey toward confident speaking.

Remember, dismantling speech anxiety is not an overnight conquest but a gradual journey. It's about building resilience, cultivating a positive mindset, and arming yourself with tools to navigate the turbulent waters of nervousness. Each strategy and technique is a brick in the foundation of your confidence, slowly dismantling the walls of fear that inhibit your potential.

Cultivating Confidence through Mindset

Confidence is more than just a cloak worn by the lucky few; it is a mindset that can be fostered and maintained by purposeful effort and steadfast conviction in oneself. The mind is the basis of confidence, and it is here that we will go on a revolutionary adventure.

Accepting Affirmations

Affirmations are self-belief seeds planted in the rich soil of your mind. They are assertions that shape your world, not simply language. Begin by finding affirmations that are relevant to your aims and desires. Phrases like "I am a confident and compelling speaker" or "My words have the power to inspire and captivate" give you confidence.

Consistency is essential. Repeat these affirmations on a daily basis, not as hollow platitudes but as profound truths. Allow them to infiltrate your brain, rewiring the narratives that govern your degree of confidence. Over time, these affirmations transform from ordinary statements to guiding concepts that shape your ideas and behaviors.

Using Visualization to Your Advantage

Visualization is the blank canvas on which your aspirations and goals are painted. Close your eyes and imagine yourself confidently standing on stage. Consider the audience hanging on your every word, their expressions filled with interest and respect. Consider yourself speaking smoothly, your message striking a deep chord with each listener.

Visualization goes beyond the confines of the imagination, it's a preparation for success. Engage all of your senses while you visualize. Feel the warmth of the limelight, hear the acclaim, and appreciate the feelings that come with success. This exercise not only prepares your head but also your subconscious mind to materialize the reality you desire.

Practical Exercises for Building Confidence Blocks

Building confidence is similar to working out a muscle in that it involves regular effort and exercise. Participate in practical activities designed to boost your confidence:

Affirmations in the Mirror: Stand in front of a mirror and state your confidence aloud. As you reinforce good thoughts about yourself, you will notice a change in your posture, demeanor, and self-assurance.

Gradual Exposure: Gradually introduce yourself to public speaking circumstances. Begin with easy environments and progressively increase the difficulty. Your confidence will grow with each successful encounter.

Document and evaluate: Record yourself giving speeches or giving presentations. Examine your strengths and areas for development. Seeing your improvement boosts your confidence in your talents.

Role-Playing: Put yourself in the shoes of a confident speaker. Take on the characteristics and mannerisms of speakers you admire. Emulating confidence progressively instills it in you.

Mindfulness and Relaxation: Before speaking engagements, practice relaxation techniques such as deep breathing or meditation. A confident mind is one that is tranquil.

Building an Unshakable Wall of Self-Belief

The journey from self-doubt to unwavering self-belief begins with the development of a resilient attitude. Affirmations instill positivity in your mind, visualization paints the picture of your accomplishment, and practical exercises develop your confidence muscle.

This path isn't about putting up a fake front of confidence; it's about discovering your own underlying confidence. It's about connecting your thoughts, emotions, and actions with the steadfast idea that you have the ability to influence, inspire, and captivate.

Remember, it's not about eradicating times of doubt, but about embracing them as stepping stones towards progress as you build this unbreakable wall of self-belief. Accept the trip, celebrate your accomplishments, and watch as your thinking transforms into an anchor that keeps you steady in the face of uncertainty.

Each speaking opportunity is a chance for me to connect authentically with my audience.

CHAPTER 2: CREATING ENGAGING CONTENT

"The most powerful words you can say to someone else are 'me too.' Mandy Hale

The Elements of an Effective Speech

Making a compelling speech is analogous to creating a masterpiece, an orchestra of words, ideas, and emotions organized to strike a deep chord with your audience. It all starts with comprehending the fundamentals:

Flow and Structure: Investigate the form of an effective speech, starting with a fascinating introduction that hooks your audience, and then moving on to a structured body that reveals your important ideas, and concluding with a memorable conclusion that reinforces your message.

Simplicity and clarity: Accept the importance of clarity in the information you provide. Simplify complicated ideas without losing their meaning. To emphasize your views, use vivid visuals and relatable experiences.

Audience Resonance: Tailor your content according to your audience's needs, interests, and objectives. Determine their pain spots, goals and then tailor your message to precisely target them.

Developing Your Storytelling Skills

The lifeblood of effective communication is storytelling—a conduit that connects the speaker and the audience. Explore the subtleties of storytelling:

Emotional Connection: Create storylines that elicit emotions. Accept the power of relevant tales, personal experiences, or instances that hit your audience's emotions.

Narrative Arc: Create a captivating narrative arc is an opening that sets the tone, a conflict that holds the reader's attention, a resolution that provides insight, and a conclusion that leaves an impression.

Authenticity and Vulnerability: Share genuine narratives about vulnerability. Authenticity fosters connection, creating a relationship between the speaker and the listener.

Utilizing Humor and Wit

Humor adds flavor to a speech, making it more appetizing and remembered. Understand how to use comedy effectively:

Appropriateness and relevance: Incorporate comedy that is appropriate for your message and audience. Check that it is acceptable and does not overpower the main contents.

Timing and Delivery: Master the timing of your humor such as the use of punch lines, stories, or funny remarks should be delivered on time, improving engagement rather than distracting from your message.

Reliability and Universality: Use relevant and universal humor. Humor that connects with your audience's experiences builds a stronger bond.

Developing Your Unique Voice

Your voice is a reflection of your personality, values, and convictions. Discover your distinct voice inside your content:

Authentic Expression: Include your true self in your material. Allow your enthusiasm and conviction to flow through your remarks.

Consistency and Clarity: Keep your messaging and communication style consistent. The effect of your information is enhanced by clarity and coherence.

Changing Your Look

Refine and modify your speaking style on a regular basis. Maintain your fundamental voice while adapting to new audiences.

Crafting interesting content is an art form that combines structure, storytelling finesse, comedy, and your own voice. In this chapter, we've looked at the foundations of effective speeches, the power of narrative, the art of comedy, and the significance of creating your own voice—all of which are critical to engaging and persuading your audience.

The path to being a confident speaker goes beyond speaking abilities; it is dependent on creating elements that not only educates but also inspires, resonates, and leaves an everlasting impact on the hearts and minds of your audience.

CHAPTER 3: MASTERING DELIVERY TECHNIQUES

"It's not what you say; it's how you say it."

Unknown

The Flexibility of Effective Speaking Styles

Effective speaking is the canvas woven with many styles, with each thread adding to a distinct and effective presentation. Let examine the various types of speaking styles:

Persuasive Speaking: Create arguments, use rhetoric, and appeal to emotions to persuade and influence your audience to your point of view.

Informative Speaking: Concentrate on educating and enlightening your audience. Present facts, insights, and information in a straightforward and structured fashion.

Inspiring Speaking: Infuse your speech with passion, enthusiasm, and inspiring anecdotes to inspire and elicit emotions, promoting action or change.

Understanding the unique characteristics of each style helps you to modify your delivery to varied circumstances and audience preferences, increasing the impact of your message.

Connecting with your Target Audience through Voice Modulation and Body Language

Voice Modulation

Learn to use your voice as a strong tool for evoking emotions, emphasizing crucial ideas, and maintaining audience involvement.

Change your tone and pitch to portray passion, seriousness, or empathy. Create a rhythm that captivates your audience by using pauses for emphasis.

To add dynamism to your voice, control your volume and tempo. Accelerate for excitement or decelerate for emphasis and seriousness.

Body Language

Your body communicates a lot; utilize it to supplement and strengthen your vocal message.

Maintain an erect and confident stance and gestures. Use deliberate motions that correspond to your voice to improve the clarity and impact of your message.

Make direct eye contact with your audience. It promotes connection, trustworthiness, and participation.

Mastering voice modulation and body language enhances your message's delivery, making it more interesting, relevant, and convincing.

Making Use of Space and Stage Presence

Space perception Awareness: The stage is your artwork; use it to command attention and make an impression. Own the stage with charm and honesty, exuding confidence and authority.

Stage Movement: Move across the stage strategically to engage different portions of the audience. Use movement to highlight significant spots or transitions.

Utilization of Props and Visual Aids: Use props or visual aids strategically to strengthen your message. They augment your material by acting as reinforcement tools.

Energy and excitement: Bring energy and excitement to your presentation. Your enthusiasm is contagious, and the audience is drawn into your world.

Adaptation to Location: Adapt your presence to the venue whether it's a vast auditorium or a small, intimate setting, altering your presence strengthens your relationship with the audience.

Learning delivery strategies requires a multifaceted strategy that includes different speaking styles, voice modulation, body language, and stage presence. Each aspect adds to the artistry of effective communication, helping you to connect, engage, and inspire your audience as well as transmit information.

You can transform your presentation into an immersive experience by understanding the versatility of speaking styles, harnessing the power of voice modulation and body language, and utilizing space and stage presence.

CHAPTER 4: ENGAGING YOUR AUDIENCE

"The way you overcome shyness is to become so wrapped up in something that you forget to be afraid."

Claudia Altucher

Interactive Techniques for Maximum Impact

The key element of good communication is engagement which is a continuous interaction that converts passive listeners into active participants. Let's delve into interactive strategies that encourage participation:

- Encourage audience engagement using interactive components. Include polls, surveys, or open-ended questions to engage your audience and elicit their opinions and perspectives.
- Break up the monotony by arranging group activities or conversations. Make opportunities for your audience to collaborate, share ideas, and learn from one another.
- Incorporate your audience into your tale. Share relatable stories that speak to their experiences, allowing people to emotionally invest in your message.

Using interactive approaches changes your presentation from a monologue to a discussion, creating a complete experience that captivates as well as engages your audience.

Question and Answer Session: Turning Obstacles into Opportunities

The Q&A session is a critical juncture—an opportunity to clarify doubts, increase knowledge, and reinforce your message. Effectively navigate Q&A sessions:

Anticipation and preparation: Anticipate likely inquiries and prepare succinct, eloquent replies. Addressing issues ahead of time improves your credibility and poise throughout the discussion.

Empathy and Active Listening: Pay close attention to each question, displaying empathy and respect for the audience member. Recognize their inquiries, ensuring that everyone feels heard and respected.

Graceful Handling of Difficulties: Approach difficult or unexpected inquiries with grace and calm. If you are unsure, be honest and offer to follow up later with a thorough response.

A well-managed Q&A session not only answers questions, but it also reinforces your knowledge and connection with the audience.

The Use of Visual Aids and Technology

Visual aids and technology operate as catalysts, enhancing the impact and clarity of your message:

- Use visuals, such as info graphics, charts, or photos, to supplement your narrative. Visuals communicate complicated information clearly and resonate with visual learners.

- Use technology to improve involvement. Use presentation tools, interactive software, or live demonstrations to make your speech more dynamic and interactive.

- Ensure that visual aids are basic, clear, and relevant. Avoid overloading the audience with too much information or intricate images that detract from your message.

By intelligently using visual aids and technology, you increase comprehension, engagement, and retention of your message.

Engaging your audience requires a deliberate combination of interactive approaches, skilled handling of Q&A sessions, and efficient integration of visual aids and technology. These aspects turn your presentation into an interactive experience—a discourse that welcomes participation, promotes dialogue, and uses multimedia to support your point.

You can create an immersive experience that captivates, informs, and inspires your audience by adopting interactive approaches, managing Q&A sessions with elegance, and leveraging visual aids and technology.

I am a continuous learner, refining my speaking skills with every experience.

CHAPTER 5: MANAGING NERVES AND DEVELOPING CONFIDENCE

Techniques for Dealing with Pre-Speech Nerves

Pre speech flutters are a natural companion on the path of public speaking, it is a mix of enthusiasm and nervousness that may either impede or drive your performance.

Let's look into ways for navigating and harnessing these jitters:
Preparation and Rehearsal: To boost your confidence, prepare diligently. Rehearse your speech several times, becoming acquainted with the subject until it becomes second nature. Practice builds familiarity and self-assurance.

Visualization and Positive Affirmations: To visualize success, use visualization techniques. Imagine yourself giving a brilliant speech that captivates your audience. Use positive affirmations to boost your confidence and believe in your talents.

Controlled Breathing and Relaxation: Before your speech, practice deep breathing and relaxation techniques. Slow, deep breaths assist to relieve stress and settle anxieties, allowing you to approach the stage calmly.

Emphasis on the Message and Audience Engagement: Turn your attention away from yourself and toward your message and audience. Focus on providing value to your audience, engaging them, and giving knowledge or insights that can help them.

Using these tactics turns pre-speech jitters into a stepping stone, transforming anxious energy into a spark for a great performance.

Strategies for Success while Cultivating Confidence

Confidence is the foundation of effective speaking, and it is developed through focused practice and a resilient mentality. Look into the following ways for improving and strengthening your confidence:

Self-Awareness and Acceptance: Recognize your own strengths and places for development. Accept your individuality and flaws, knowing that they add to your original voice.

Incremental Challenges and Successes: Push yourself progressively. Every successful speaking engagement, no matter the size, boosts confidence. Celebrate achievements, no matter how minor they appear.

Continuous Learning and Growth mentality: Adopt a growth mentality, which is the concept that talents can be developed through devotion and hard effort. Accept every speaking opportunity as a chance to learn and improve.

Positive Reinforcement and Self-Reflection: Acknowledge your successes and growth. Following your speech, engage in self-reflection.

Engage in self-reflection post-speech, identifying areas of improvement while acknowledging your achievements. Navigating nerves and building confidence is a transformative journey which is a fusion of managing pre-speech jitters, cultivating unshakable confidence, and learning from the wealth of speaking experiences. By mastering techniques to manage nerves, embracing strategies for confidence cultivation, and learning from the lessons experience offers, you evolve into a resilient and impactful speaker.

My presence on stage is confident,

and my body language reinforces my

message.

CHAPTER 6: LEARNING FROM EXPERIENCE

Experience is the best teacher, a storehouse of lessons, insights, and possibilities for progress. Accept the benefit of learning from your speaking experiences:

- Think about previous speaking events. Examine what worked well, places for growth, and lessons learned. Use this information to improve your future performances.
- Seek input from trustworthy peers, mentors, or audience members. Constructive criticism gives vital views and places for improvement.
- Consider setbacks to be stepping stones to greater success. Accept times of discomfort or blunders as drivers for growth, resilience, and adaptation.
- Adapt your speaking style based on past experiences. Continually evolve and refine your approach, integrating lessons learned into your repertoire.
- Learning from experience fosters continual improvement, refinement of skills, and the evolution of your speaking prowess.

Case Studies and Lessons from Successful Speakers

Winston Churchill: The Power of Resilience in Speech

Winston Churchill's speeches during World War II epitomize the power of resilience. Facing adversity, he delivered resounding speeches that instilled hope, determination, and unity. His ability to craft messages that rallied a nation, despite challenging circumstances, showcases the importance of adaptability and determination in effective speaking.

Lesson Learned: Adversity can be transformed into opportunity. Resilience and adaptability are crucial in crafting impactful speeches, especially during challenging times.

Maya Angelou: The Art of Authenticity in Storytelling

Maya Angelou's poignant storytelling and raw authenticity resonate deeply with audiences. Through her experiences, she shared stories that touched hearts and inspired change. Her unwavering commitment to authenticity illustrates the power of vulnerability and honesty in connecting with an audience.

Lesson Learned: Authenticity is magnetic. Embrace vulnerability and honesty in storytelling as it fosters genuine connections and leaves a lasting impact.

Steve Jobs: Crafting Compelling Presentations through Simplicity

Steve Jobs was a master of simplicity in presentations. His iconic product launches were marked by minimalistic yet powerful presentations. He distilled complex ideas into simple, compelling messages, emphasizing clarity and elegance in communication.

Lesson Learned: Less is more. Simplify complex ideas to make them accessible and memorable. Clarity and conciseness elevate the impact of your message.

Real-Life Examples: Practical Application of Techniques

Michelle Obama's "Let's Move!"Campaign: Audience-Centric Communication

Michelle Obama's campaign focused on combating childhood obesity, "Let's Move!", was a testament to audience-centric communication. Her speeches resonated with parents, educators, and children, tailoring messages to address the specific needs and concerns of each group.

Practical Application: Understanding your target audience is crucial. Tailor your content to address their needs, aspirations, and pain points, fostering a deeper connection.

TED Talks: Engaging through Storytelling and Impactful Delivery

TED Talks exemplify the power of storytelling and impactful delivery. Speakers often weave narratives that captivate, inform, and inspire. Their delivery, coupled with compelling storytelling, hooks audiences and delivers memorable messages.

Practical Application: Incorporate storytelling and engaging delivery techniques into your speeches. Create narratives which feel true, elicit emotions, and leave a lasting impact.

Elon Musk's Presentations: Merging Vision with Technological Innovation

Elon Musk's presentations blend vision with technological innovation. His ability to articulate futuristic visions while simplifying complex technological concepts makes his presentations compelling and accessible to a wide audience.

Practical Application: Articulate a clear vision while simplifying complex ideas. Translate technical jargon into accessible language to engage diverse audiences.

Learning from outstanding speakers via case studies and real-life examples provides vital insights and practical applications in the field of public speaking. The experiences of renowned speakers such as Winston Churchill, Maya Angelou, Steve Jobs, Michelle Obama, and Elon Musk serve as guides, providing lessons in perseverance, sincerity, simplicity, audience-centric communication, compelling delivery, and imaginative articulation.

Gaining knowledge of audience engagement methods involves deconstructing and extracting insights from their approaches. Real-world examples demonstrate how these skills can be used in compelling presentations. These lessons can be incorporated into your speaking journey to elevate communication, inspire change, and leave an indelible mark.

Every speaking engagement is an opportunity for growth, and I embrace it with passion and determination.

CHAPTER 7: THE ETHICAL SPEAKER

Authenticity, Integrity, and Trust in Public Speaking

The ethical speaker's compass is a moral basis that underlies every spoken word, ensuring honesty, integrity, and trustworthiness in communication.

Authenticity in Expression: The cornerstone of ethical speaking is authenticity. It requires synchronizing your words, actions, and beliefs in order to show your true self to your audience. Authentic speakers establish real relationships with their audiences by remaining true to themselves and their message.

Communication Integrity: Communication integrity is the foundation of ethical communication. Maintaining honesty, openness, and moral standards provides consistency and credibility of the speaker's message. Integrity builds trust and credibility, creating the framework for long-term connections with your audience.

Building Trust: Trust is built via continuous ethical behavior and open communication. Ethical speakers place a premium on honesty, dependability, and responsibility, building a bond of trust and respect with their audience.

Persuasion and Honesty in Balance

Persuasion is frequently used in public speaking, requiring a fine balance between influencing ideas and retaining honesty and integrity.

Ethical Persuasion: Ethical speakers attempt to influence their audiences with honesty and respect for their autonomy. They give persuasive arguments based on facts, logic, and ethical reasoning, while avoiding manipulation or deception.

Honesty in Messaging: Honesty is the bedrock of ethical persuasion. Speakers must present information truthfully and accurately, acknowledging differing perspectives while maintaining the ethical obligation to present a balanced and truthful narrative.

Transparency and Disclosure: Transparent communication builds trust. Ethical speakers disclose biases, conflicts of interest, or limitations in their expertise, ensuring transparency in their messaging.

Upholding Ethical Standards

- Ethical speakers prioritize accuracy and fact-check their content rigorously. Verifying information before presenting it to the audience upholds ethical standards and credibility.

- Respect for diverse perspectives is integral to ethical communication. Ethical speakers acknowledge and respect differing viewpoints, fostering an inclusive and respectful environment for dialogue.

- Speakers bear a responsibility for the influence they wield. Ethical speakers use their platform responsibly, considering the potential impact of their words and actions on their audience and society as a whole.

The ethical speaker operates within the realm of authenticity, integrity, and trust, maintaining a delicate equilibrium between persuasion and honesty. Upholding ethical standards ensures that their communication is grounded in truthfulness, transparency, and respect for their audience's autonomy.

Ethical public speaking involves authenticity, integrity, and trust, fostering meaningful connections with audiences. Balancing persuasion with honesty involves presenting compelling arguments, maintaining transparency, and respecting diverse perspectives. This approach not only enhances credibility and trust but also impacts the message's impact on the audience.

I am a compelling storyteller, engaging my audience with impactful narratives.

CHAPTER 8: ELEVATING YOUR SPEAKING JOURNEY

Continual Improvement through Practice

- Getting better at public speaking starts with careful and concentrated practice. Regularly push yourself by speaking in a variety of situations, whether small meetings, seminars, or major conferences. Each speaking experience is a chance for development and refining.

- Feedback is a driving force for progress. After each speaking engagement, actively seek feedback from mentors, peers, or audience members. Accept constructive criticism since it might help you improve your craft.

- Make a recording of your talks or presentations. Reviewing your performances allows you to examine your body language, tone, tempo, and information delivery, which helps you find areas for development. Self-evaluation is a valuable tool for ongoing development.

- Invest in your speaking abilities by attending workshops, seminars, or joining public speaking organizations such as Toastmasters. Continuous study and skill improvement are essential for improving your speaking abilities.

Leveraging Public Speaking for Personal Branding and Networking

- **Developing Your Personal Brand:** Public speaking is an effective method for developing your personal brand. Craft a unique speaking style that aligns with your expertise and values. Consistently delivering valuable content enhances your reputation, positioning you as an authority in your field.

- **Networking Opportunities:** Speaking engagements provide networking avenues. Engage with fellow speakers, organizers, and audience members. Networking fosters connections, opens doors to collaborations, and expands your professional circle.

- **Establishing Thought Leadership:** Use speaking opportunities to share your expertise and insights. Offering valuable content positions you as a thought leader, attracting like-minded individuals and potential collaborators seeking your expertise.

- **Online Presence and Visibility:** Leverage digital platforms to amplify your speaking journey. Share highlights of your presentations, insights, and speaking engagements on social media or professional networks. A strong online presence increases your visibility and reach.

Elevating your speaking journey is a multifaceted endeavor encompassing continual improvement through practice and leveraging public speaking for personal branding and networking. By committing to deliberate practice, seeking feedback, and engaging in professional development, you continuously refine your speaking skills, ensuring a trajectory of growth and refinement.

Public speaking is a powerful tool for personal branding, networking, and professional advancement. It involves crafting a unique brand, leveraging online visibility, and continuously refining skills to leave a lasting impact.

I embrace nerves as a sign of excitement and readiness to deliver an impactful speech.

CONCLUSION: YOUR JOURNEY TO BECOMING A CONFIDENT SPEAKER

Your journey to becoming a confident speaker in 2024 has been a transformative expedition—an odyssey marked by growth, learning, and continuous evolution. From the initial steps of understanding the foundational elements of public speaking to navigating nerves, building confidence, and refining your craft, each chapter has contributed to your metamorphosis into a captivating and influential speaker.

Your journey began with a profound understanding of the fundamental elements of effective public speaking. From laying the foundation of impactful content creation to mastering delivery techniques and engaging your audience, you acquired the tools necessary to craft compelling messages and captivate your listeners. The journey to confidence was a pivotal phase, marked by the dismantling of speech anxiety, the cultivation of an unshakable mindset, and the embracement of experience as a catalyst for growth.

Strategies, techniques, and real-life examples from influential speakers guided you in navigating nerves, harnessing resilience, and embracing authenticity—a journey that fortified your confidence and authenticity as a speaker.

The speaker's ethical journey in public speaking involves values of authenticity, integrity, and trust. They balance persuasion with honesty, upholding ethical standards, and respecting diverse perspectives. They continuously improve through practice, feedback integration, and leveraging speaking engagements for personal branding and networking. Each opportunity helps establish thought leadership, build a personal brand, and expand professional networks.

Reflecting on your journey in speaking, it's crucial to acknowledge the transformative impact on professional and personal growth. Your transformation from a hesitant speaker to a confident communicator demonstrates dedication, resilience, and commitment to excellence. Remember that your journey evolves, and embrace each speaking opportunity for further growth and connection.

Your influence extends beyond the words you speak. It permeates through the connections you forge, the knowledge you impart, and the inspiration you instill in your audience. Your voice becomes a catalyst for change, a source of empowerment, and a beacon of authenticity in a world hungry for genuine and impactful communication.

In 2024, be confident in your speaking abilities, recognizing that confidence is a lifelong journey of growth, adaptation, and influence. Embrace challenges as opportunities, celebrate victories as milestones, and cherish connections formed through your words. Your journey will pave the way for impactful communication, authenticity, and unwavering influence.

In this new era of speaking, may your voice resonate, your message inspire, and your journey as a confident speaker in 2024 pave the way for a future marked by impactful communication, authenticity, and unwavering influence.

I radiate enthusiasm, energizing my audience and creating a positive atmosphere.

PREPARATION	
MY TOPIC	
TITLE OF SPEECH/PRESENTATION	
TARGETED AUDIENCE	
PURPOSE OF SPEECH	
POSSIBLE SOURCES OF INFORMATION	

SPEECH /PRESENTATION OUTLINE

PREPARATION	
MY TOPIC	
TITLE OF SPEECH/PRESENTATION	
TARGETED AUDIENCE	
PURPOSE OF SPEECH	

SPEECH /PRESENTATION OUTLINE

POSSIBLE SOURCES OF INFORMATION	

PREPARATION	
MY TOPIC	
TITLE OF SPEECH/PRESENTATION	
TARGETED AUDIENCE	
PURPOSE OF SPEECH	
POSSIBLE SOURCES OF INFORMATION	

PREPARATION	
MY TOPIC	
TITLE OF SPEECH/PRESENTATION	
TARGETED AUDIENCE	
PURPOSE OF SPEECH	
POSSIBLE SOURCES OF INFORMATION	

PREPARATION	
MY TOPIC	
TITLE OF SPEECH/PRESENTATION	
TARGETED AUDIENCE	
PURPOSE OF SPEECH	
POSSIBLE SOURCES OF INFORMATION	

PREPARATION	
MY TOPIC	
TITLE OF SPEECH/PRESENTATION	
TARGETED AUDIENCE	
PURPOSE OF SPEECH	
POSSIBLE SOURCES OF INFORMATION	

PREPARATION	
MY TOPIC	
TITLE OF SPEECH/PRESENTATION	
TARGETED AUDIENCE	
PURPOSE OF SPEECH	
POSSIBLE SOURCES OF INFORMATION	

PREPARATION	
MY TOPIC	
TITLE OF SPEECH/PRESENTATION	
TARGETED AUDIENCE	
PURPOSE OF SPEECH	
POSSIBLE SOURCES OF INFORMATION	

www.ingramcontent.com/pod-product-compliance
Lightning Source LLC
Chambersburg PA
CBHW060003300526
45794CB00003B/1064